D1030947

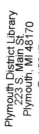

Ridiculous
RIDDLES

By **Cyl Lee**

BIG BUDDY

JOKES

Big Buddy Books
An imprint of Abdo Publishing
abdopublishing.com

abdopublishing.com

Published by Abdo Publishing, a division of ABDO, PO Box 398166, Minneapolis, Minnesota 55439.
Copyright © 2017 by Abdo Consulting Group, Inc. International copyrights reserved in all countries.
No part of this book may be reproduced in any form without written permission from the publisher.
Big Buddy Books™ is a trademark and logo of Abdo Publishing.

Printed in the United States of America, North Mankato, Minnesota.
082016
012017

THIS BOOK CONTAINS
RECYCLED MATERIALS

Illustrations: Sunny Grey/Spectrum Studio

Coordinating Series Editor: Tamara L. Britton
Contributing Editor: Katie Lajiness
Graphic Design: Taylor Higgins

Publisher's Cataloging-in-Publication Data

Names: Lee, Cyl, author.
Title: Ridiculous riddles / by Cyl Lee.
Description: Minneapolis, MN : Abdo Publishing, 2017. | Series: Big buddy jokes
Identifiers: LCCN 2016944872 | ISBN 9781680785159 (lib. bdg.) | ISBN
    9781680798753 (ebook)
Subjects: LCSH: Wit and humor--Juvenile humor.
Classification: DDC 818/.602--dc23
LC record available at http://lccn.loc.gov/2016944872

A butcher is 6'4" tall, wears size 3XL pants and size 12 shoes. What does he weigh?

Meat!

What cannot be seen, but only heard, and will not speak unless spoken to?

An echo!

A rooster was sitting on the peak of a roof. He laid an egg. Which way did the egg roll down the roof?

It didn't! Roosters don't lay eggs!

What word is spelled incorrectly in the dictionary?

Incorrectly.

Johnny's mom has three children. One is named April, and another is named May. What is the last child's name?

Johnny.

What is white when it's dirty and black when it's clean?

A blackboard!

When is a door not a door?

When it's ajar!

What belongs to you but is used more often by others?

Your name.

How many months have 28 days?

All of them!

What's the best way to make a pair of pants last?

Make the coat first.

What two things can't you have for breakfast?

Lunch and dinner!

The more there is of it, the less you see. What is it?

Darkness!

Rich people need it. Poor people have it. If you eat it you will die. What is it?

Nothing!

9

Where do frogs go to get their glasses?

To the hop-tometrist!

On the way to the water hole a zebra met six giraffes. Each giraffe had three monkeys hanging from its neck. Each monkey had two birds on its tail. How many animals were going to the water hole?

One — the zebra.

What has a face and two hands, but no arms or legs?

A clock.

What starts with *E*, ends with *E* and contains one letter?

An envelope.

What travels around the world while sitting in a corner?

A stamp.

What gets wetter the more it dries?

A towel.

Can you name five days of the week without saying Sunday, Monday, Tuesday, Wednesday, Thursday, Friday, or Saturday?

The day before yesterday, yesterday, today, tomorrow, the day after tomorrow.

What is a broken down hot rod?

A shot rod!

What is full of holes but can still hold water?

A sponge!

On your way to school, you count 20 houses on your right, and on your way home you count 20 houses on your left, how many total houses have you counted?

Twenty!

The more you take, the more you leave behind. What are they?

Footsteps.

What has a big mouth but can't talk?

A jar.

Trouble.

16

What runs but never walks?

Water!

What question can you never answer "yes" to?

"Are you asleep?"

You throw away the outside, cook the inside, eat the outside, and throw away the inside. What vegetable is it?

Corn on the cob!

What is the beginning of eternity, the end of time and space, the beginning of every end, and the end of every race?

The letter *E*.

What starts with *T*, ends with *T*, and is full of tea?

A teapot!

What can you give away and still keep?

A cold!

A snowball!

19

What has no beginning, no end and nothing in the middle?

A doughnut!

What gets harder to catch the faster you run?

Your breath!

A man rode to town on his horse Friday. The next day he rode back on Friday. How is this possible?

His horse's name is Friday!

What is always coming but never arrives?

Tomorrow.

What nails do carpenters hate to hit?

Fingernails!

How can you name the capital of every US state in two seconds?

Washington, DC!

What rises up in the morning and waves all day?

A flag.

When are houses like books?

When they have stories in them.

There are two US coins that equal 30 cents. One of them is not a nickel. How is this possible?

There is a quarter and a nickel. The quarter is the one that's not a nickel.

What two words have the most letters?

Post office!

I run but I never walk. I have a mouth but I never talk. I have a bed but I never lie. What am I?

A river.

What did the traffic light say to the driver?

Don't look! I'm changing!

Who can shave all day and still have a beard?

A barber.

What goes up but never comes down?

Your age.

Why did the girl smear peanut butter on the road?

To go with the traffic jam.

26

What time do most people go to the dentist?

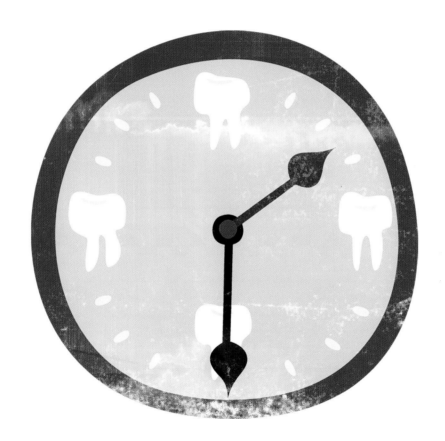

Tooth hurty!

Who earns a living by driving customers away?

A taxi driver!

Which flower talks the most?

Tulips because they have two lips.

Everyone has it and no one can lose it. What is it?

A shadow.

What goes up when rain comes down?

An umbrella!

I am found in the sea and on land, but I do not walk or swim. I travel by foot, but I am toeless. I'm never far from home. What am I?

A snail.

I don't have wings, but I can fly. I don't have eyes, but I will cry! What am I?

A cloud.

What grows larger the more you take away?

A hole!

What is filled every morning and emptied every night, except once a year when it is filled at night and emptied in the morning?

A stocking!

WEBSITES

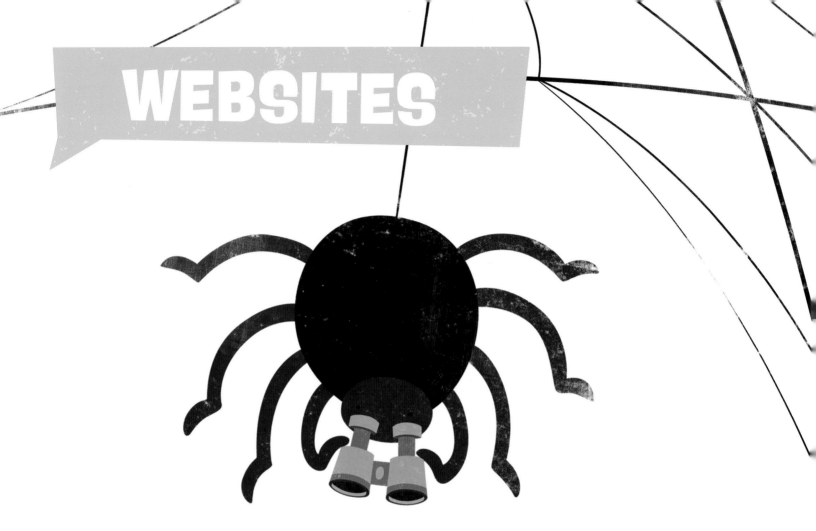

To learn more about Big Buddy Jokes, visit **booklinks.abdopublishing.com.** These links are routinely monitored and updated to provide the most current information available.